## ACKNOWLEDGEMENT

For Taunya.

Belief is powerful.

Action is undeniable.

Love is unconditional.

## ABOUT THE AUTHOR

Michael is currently Associate Professor of Social Work at Tennessee State University in Nashville, TN. A former Master of Social Work program director, Wright has taught a diverse population of students at both the baccalaureate and master degree levels.

His other research interests include trauma and resilience, complex adaptive systems, and entrepreneurship. Wright has also been a macro practice consultant more than 12 years for public and private entities seeking capacity, social research, leadership training, and educational media creation.

**Succeed @ www.mawmedia.com**

# Interviewing Skills: Introduction to GIM+

By Michael A. Wright, PhD, LAPSW

MAWMedia Group

Nashville TN

Wright, Michael A.

Copyright Page

This text in its entirety is © 2012 by Michael A. Wright (michael@mawmedia.com). This text is produced for sale and should not be copied without the purchase of a valid usage license. Licenses and supplementary products are available at MAWMedia.com.

Interviewing Skills: Introduction to GIM+

By Michael A. Wright, PhD, LAPSW

**First Edition**
July 2012

ISBN: 978-0-9842170-5-2

# GIM+ Introduction

## CLASS ASSIGNMENTS

1. Compose an **ANALYSIS OF YOURSELF** describing your communication styles and attitudes.
2. Utilize the Analysis of Yourself as a basis for **AN INTERVIEW SCRIPT** dramatizing all GIM+ skills.
    a. Create a four-column table with alternating colored rows.
    b. For each of the Worker interactions, include
        i. SKILL: List the GIM+ step and the sub-skill you intend with your comment.
        ii. PURPOSE: Your professional reaction to what the client said. Based in the skill, this helps determine what you will say next.
        iii. INNER THOUGHTS: Your gut reaction based on experience and humanness. What are you thinking at this moment?
    c. For each of the Client interactions, include
        i. REACTION: Ego defense, logical fallacy, or intention of the client. List what the client is gathering from the interaction.
        ii. REASONING: The reasoning and assessment is going on within the client. The client is attempting to achieve something as well.
        iii. MEANING: What the client is thinking based on what the caseworker has said or preconceived notions.
3. Compose **TRAINING CASE REPORT**.
    a. Reflect on the Analysis and Dramatization.
    b. Describe the major challenges to achieving the change.
    c. Detail the process learning
    d. Articulate the self-learning that resulted from your dramatization
    e. List lessons that other workers can learn from your experience.

## Full **ANALYSIS OF YOURSELF** Outline

A. Create a Profile of yourself. Describe the person and pertinent characteristics that aid in contextualizing the story. Examples of context include description of neighborhood, parents' personality, significant experiences growing up, etc. if applicable. Detail the influences on your life. Provide a paragraph on your goals, heroes, achievements, and greatest fear. [PREPARATION: MY PROFILE]

B. Detail your ego defenses, logical fallacies, values, and beliefs. [ENGAGEMENT: THE REAL ME]

C. Articulate what an interviewer would need to inquire about in order to fully know you. Present the person's perceptions of their own thinking processes, intentions, and influences. Compare those to any corroborating information from other people, news or historical documentation, or other sources. [ASSESSMENT: MY PERCEPTIONS]

D. Develop at least one clearly stated hypothesis toward changing your relationship with someone or something. The hypothesis should take the form: If I change [some aspect of myself], it would change my relationship with [someone or something] for the better. [PLANNING: MY OPTIONS]

E. Conduct a review of scholarly literature to examine the hypothesis posed. [IMPLEMENTATION: REPORTING ON ME]

F. In light of the literature review, analyze yourself to further articulate the barriers, inconsistencies, and failures along with your strengths, learning, and increased self-awareness resulting from the change process. [EVALUATION: ME IN CONTEXT]

G. Analyze the narrative you have created thus far for themes that surface. Use these to build a theoretical model of intervention that you could train others to use in interacting with you. [TERMINATION: ME AS EXAMPLE]

H. Reflect on the value of a community in which citizens examine and rehearse self-examination. List potential responses to scarcity, conflict, and disease. Discuss how interactions between citizens can support sustainable outcomes in mental and physical health. [FOLLOW-UP: ME IN COMMUNITY]

# GIM+ Introduction

Table of Contents

**GIM+ Bibliographic Acknowledgements .......................................... 9**
**Overview of GIM+ .................................................................... 11**
**Preparation ............................................................................. 14**
    ATTITUDES ........................................................................... 14
        *Self-Awareness: Being a Good Mirror .................................... 14*
        *Self-Awareness: Ego Defenses and Logical Fallacies ................ 14*
        *Attitudes: Use of Self & Environment .................................... 15*
    BEHAVIORS ........................................................................... 20
        *Examine Self in Relationship to the Client ............................. 20*
        *Resist Countertransference .................................................. 20*
        *Focus on the Presenting Problem not Personal Lifestyle ........... 20*
**Engagement ............................................................................ 22**
    ATTITUDES ........................................................................... 22
        *Attraction ......................................................................... 22*
        *Judgment .......................................................................... 22*
        *Discrimination .................................................................. 23*
        *Competence ...................................................................... 23*
    BEHAVIORS ........................................................................... 24
        *Initiate Rapport ................................................................ 24*
        *Orient the Client to the Helping Process ................................ 24*
        *Articulate Your Professional Role ........................................ 25*
        *List the Agency Services ..................................................... 26*
        *List the Client Expectations ................................................ 26*
        *Identify the Presenting Problem .......................................... 27*
**Assessment ............................................................................. 28**
    ATTITUDES ........................................................................... 28
        *Strengths & Resilience ....................................................... 28*
        *Cultural Competence ......................................................... 30*
    TECHNIQUE: NOTING ............................................................. 32
    BEHAVIORS ........................................................................... 33

  *Probing* ........................................................................................... *34*
  *Reflecting* ....................................................................................... *34*

## Planning .................................................................................... **38**
 ATTITUDES ............................................................................................ 38
  *Client Primacy* .............................................................................. *38*
  *Data-based Action Plan & Client Agreement* ............................. *39*
 TECHNIQUE: EVALUATE GOAL STRUCTURE ........................................ 39
 BEHAVIORS ........................................................................................... 40
  *Connect with Services* ................................................................... *40*
  *Translate Into Goals* ..................................................................... *41*
  *Contract with the Client* ............................................................... *42*

## Implementation ....................................................................... **44**
 ATTITUDES ............................................................................................ 44
  *Empowerment: Permission, Perspective & Options* ..................... *44*
 BEHAVIORS ........................................................................................... 45
  *Focusing* ........................................................................................ *45*
  *Advising* ........................................................................................ *46*
  *Representing* .................................................................................. *46*
  *Reframing* ..................................................................................... *47*
  *Confronting* ................................................................................... *48*
  *Responding with Immediacy* ......................................................... *48*

## Evaluation ................................................................................. **50**
 ATTITUDES ............................................................................................ 50
  *Reflecting on Practice with the Client* .......................................... *50*
  *Contribute to the Professional Knowledge Base* ........................... *50*
 TECHNIQUE: SINGLE-SUBJECT DESIGN .............................................. 51
 BEHAVIORS ........................................................................................... 52
  *Scaling* .......................................................................................... *52*

## Termination .............................................................................. **54**
 ATTITUDES ............................................................................................ 54
  *Sensitivity to Emotional Attachment* ........................................... *54*

## GIM+ Introduction

    *Reflecting on Practice with Colleagues* ............................................................... *54*
  BEHAVIORS .................................................................................................. 54
    *Make Referral* ................................................................................................. *54*
    *Plan for Termination* ...................................................................................... *54*
    *Articulate Goal Completion* ............................................................................ *56*
    *Complete Final Evaluation* .............................................................................. *58*

**Follow-up** ............................................................................................................ **59**
  ATTITUDES .................................................................................................. 59
    *"No-Exit" Relationships* ................................................................................. *59*
  BEHAVIORS .................................................................................................. 59
    *Sponsor Relationship* ...................................................................................... *60*
    *Create Training Case* ...................................................................................... *60*

# GIM+ Bibliographic Acknowledgements

This training is informed by the work of Kirst-Ashman and Hull (2006), Cournoyer (2011), best practices in coaching, and Solution-Focused Brief Intervention (SFBI). Concepts and attitudes described in each of these are considered in creation of the "GIM Plus" (GIM+) approach. The Generalist Intervention Model (GIM) is a planned change process advanced by Kirst-Ashman and Hull (2006) in their text, <u>Understanding Generalist Practice</u>. Cournoyer describes a separate model of intervention based in social work skills. Both describe the completion of the planned change process as exit. GIM+ supports a sponsorship model that maintains the worker-client relationship beyond the interviewing interaction. Both Kirst-Ashman & Hull and Cournoyer suggest more or less linear skill development in the context of the worker-client interaction. GIM+, informed by SFBI, considers that each interaction can have non-linear application of skills. In any case, competence in interviewing to support a change process results from practice and examples. GIM+ provides both a clarified conception of the worker role and an alternative ordering of practice behaviors in the context of the skills identified by Kirst-Ashman & Hull and Cournoyer.

Kirst-Ashman and Hull discuss the impact of organizational and environmental structure on the interaction between worker and client, but Cournoyer (2008) explores this area of bias, self-awareness, and role definition in depth. GIM+ adds this process of reflection as a necessary step to be completed by the worker prior to engagement with the client.

Interviewing skills, in the context of professional practice, require tools and segues even in the presence of a solid planned change process such as GIM. Tools that keep the conversation moving with purpose have been described in many texts including Cournoyer. In GIM+, a selection of common interaction tools is ordered by the planned change process of GIM.

# GIM+ Introduction

Kirst-Ashman and Hull discuss a final step, Follow-Up, as a choice for the worker between "reassessment" and "discontinued contact." Cournoyer describes "saying goodbye." Sponsorship or coaching models may fit better in the context of an ethic toward building community. A community may house individuals who perform multiple roles including those of helper and recipient of help. Treatment compliance or sustained peak experiences are best achieved in the context of community (with sponsorship) as opposed to an individual struggle alone. GIM+ adopts an approach of interrelatedness while seeking to maintain self-determination, client primacy, and self-sufficiency. On its face, it seems increasingly difficult for the average worker to manage new cases while still maintaining meaningful contact with a growing community of clients. But, GIM+ expands beyond the "community of clients" toward actual community—embracing current community groups and support, peer mentoring, expanded worker training, and sponsorship as a maintenance activity. These are discussed further in the Evaluation, Termination, and Follow-up skills chapters.

Work with Solution-focused Brief Intervention (SFBI) suggests that the change process is a series of solutions presented enabling the client to perceive behavior choices that support her goals. SFBI in GIM+ is informed by the seminal works of Walter & Peller (1992), DeShazer & Berg (1992), and Miller & Berg (1995). This approach fits the strengths and empowerment focus of Kirst-Ashman and Hull's original GIM. GIM+ applies SFBI to suggest that the planned change process of GIM can be applied in each worker-client interaction. In this way, GIM+ enables a conception of the worker-client interaction as planned change at each interaction with increased efficacy across multiple interactions.

Empowerment information is built on the work of Hardy & Leiba-O'Sullivan (1998). They suggested a four-component definition of empowerment: resources, process, meaning and experience. Informed by operational research, the components are recast as resources, decision points, structural controls, and experience.

# Overview of GIM+

First, it must be understood that the interviewing skills described in this title support facilitation of a change process: assessment and intervention. This is not "therapy" or a "therapeutic interaction." Achievement of certain change goals may improve the mental and relational health of the client, but change process is not that of therapy. The central difference is that this generalist approach does NOT require a diagnosis, whereas traditional therapy requires diagnosis. The assessment skill in GIM+ results in clearly identified goals and an articulation of the client's perceptions of potential choices. The change process seeks to assist the client to create personal goals and steps toward goal achievement, increase the perceived choice set of the client, and empower the client to make choices that support his goals.

Therefore, the worker is termed interviewer or facilitator, not therapist or clinician. In the context of change theory, also, understand that the worker is not the change agent. The client is the change agent—the individual responsible for the achievement or delay in the change process. Consider that the worker in this model is ineffective whenever she removes the client's responsibility for success in the change process. A simple rule of thumb is to resist the need to console or make the client feel better. Consolation is an unsustainable outcome and antithetical to empowerment. This will be discussed further in the Implementation skill chapter.

GIM+ can best be understood as assessment and intervention. Assessment includes the Preparation, Engagement, Assessment and Planning skills. Intervention includes the Implementation, Evaluation, Termination, and Follow-up skills.

In GIM+, Preparation is assessment of self—self-awareness and evaluation of the worker toward the establishment of a baseline for the reflection of the client reality.

# GIM+ Introduction

Engagement allows the client to begin to assess the environment of the change process including an assessment of you, the facilitator. Engagement is primarily useful to articulate your role, clear up any misconceptions, set clear expectations, and identify the presenting problem.

Assessment can have many different implementations based on what presenting problem the client perceives and is motivated to work address. A thorough analysis will include multiple systems sizes and ecological levels with an eye on the person in her environment as well as the interactions of rules and environment on the client's perception of potential choices.

Perhaps the central learning in the planning skill is to formulate a plan based on data, incorporating the client's identified motivations, perceptions, and power. This requires the facilitator to synthesize information, prioritize, and set goals. All of this must be done with the client leading.

Implementation skills focus on empowerment of the client. Contrary to the debunked, "you can do it" model, empowerment in this skill separates beliefs, behaviors, feelings, sensations, and context to enable clear choice options by the client herself. Proper implementation skills application balances help and encouragement with challenge and self-sufficiency.

In GIM+, Evaluation skills are research methods for interviewing practice. Proper evaluation provides evidence for best practices. Sharing of outcomes gained through evaluation are valuable contributions to the professional knowledge base.

Termination, in GIM+, is the conclusion of a change process and an invitation into productive community. The approach is a "no-exit" approach, meaning that clients are encouraged to return to the interaction whenever additional support is needed. In addition, proper termination expands the support options to include others besides the facilitator alone.

Follow-up, in GIM+, operationalizes the "no-exit" community and sets up a regular schedule of connection with former clients. Former clients become a valuable resource for evaluating the long-term impact of interactions. As well, as success stories and experts, they provide an ever-expanding support pool for current and future clients.

# GIM+ Introduction

# Preparation

In GIM+, Preparation is assessment of self—self-awareness and evaluation of the worker toward the establishment of a baseline for the reflection of the client reality.

## Attitudes

**Self-Awareness: Being a Good Mirror**

The interviewing described in this title is primarily concerned with engaging a client in a change process. In order to be successful, the facilitator must gain the ability to use herself in appropriate ways to engage with the client. The facilitator does have an impact on the interaction. This impact can move the client toward self-sufficiency and successful change as the facilitator continually reflects the client's behaviors, perceptions, and choice options back to the client. This is termed "being a good mirror," allowing the client to see herself with little distortion but appropriate clarification from the facilitator. A first step toward recognizing truth in others is to identify truth within oneself. The next section will describe two important ways that humans disguise truth. Understanding ego defenses and logical fallacies will help the facilitator to address inconsistencies and bias within himself so that these do not distort the assessment of the client.

**Self-Awareness: Ego Defenses and Logical Fallacies**

**Ego Defenses**

Ego defenses are the characteristic ways that you defend yourself against primarily psychological attacks. These attacks can be real or perceived. Ego defenses are sometimes applied in unsustainable ways such as to hide the truth, but they are not inherently good or bad. The need to self-protect is a common and useful human trait. The challenge in interview facilitation is to satisfy the need for safety and equilibrium in ways that invite honesty and productive rapport. Common ego defenses include denial, displacement, intellectualization, projection, rationalization, suppression, sublimation, and counterfeiting.

As a professional, your task is to monitor your use of ego defenses. Rather than considering them to be bad or good, ask whether self-defense through a certain ego defense is useful toward your relationship goals with the client.

**Logical Fallacies**

Logical Fallacies are distortions of reality that are typically used to win an argument. As they distort reality, logical fallacies are not often useful in achieving success in any change process. Common logical fallacies include Straw Man, Slippery Slope, and Red Herring.

As a professional, logical fallacies as a means of self-defense are inappropriate on the part of the worker. Often, the worker will have opportunity to correct the logical fallacies of the client. Each opportunity should be approached with the provision of knowledge as the primary goal. It is not enough to say, "That logic is flawed." The worker must provide additional information that enables the client to re-consider her logic. For example, a client who states a slippery slope logical fallacy, "All people who drink eventually become drunkards," may benefit from a worker who counters, "Actually, studies have suggested that the factors supporting alcoholism include genes passed from parents, physiology exacerbated by stress and poor mental health, social factors like friends, and socio-environmental factors like advertising and television."

**Attitudes: Use of Self & Environment**

As worker, you have a grand impact on the experience of the client. Success in interviewing begins with knowledge of self, and extends to an awareness of the power and opportunity of the environment you create for the client. The basics to monitor are tone externals, tone internals, and attentiveness.

Tone refers to the ambience communicated by externals like lighting, position of seating, exits, and the décor of your interview location. Tone also includes internals like your voice, your dress, and your mannerisms.

## GIM+ Introduction

Consider what lighting options you have and what each communicates. Fluorescent lighting can be harsh and convey an institutional feel. Halogen or other home-like lamp lighting can invite calm and a more home-like atmosphere.

Seating conveys purpose and relationship. Sitting behind a desk separating you from the client conveys a power differential. Sitting at two similar chairs separated by a small table communicates a more equal relationship.

If it is possible, arrange the office such that you as worker and the clients have equal access to exits. This provides a sense of comfort to the hesitant client, and a sense of caution to the more aggressive client.

Consider what photos, degrees, awards and other office decorations communicate to clients. Multiple photos of family and friends can cause distraction. One framed degree can convey competence, while a wall of awards can communicate motivation to compete rather than motivation toward client success.

If you have the option, also consider how colors impact mood, communicate purpose, and offer comfort or distraction. A simple rule of thumb follows. For younger clients, you may use more, but simpler, easily identifiable colors. For adults, fewer, yet more non-standard colors are possible. Whites convey institutional settings. Blues and earth tones (brown and green) are calming. Yellows and pastels convey softness. Reds and oranges are stimulating.

### Voice

Simple rule: Keep your voice consistent with your intended communication of feeling. For most, this is a natural skill. The task is to communicate with authenticity. For others, volume and the expression of authenticity is the result of practice.

Two considerations will usually addresses the volume issue. First, speak at a level that will allow you to be heard. Work in cubicles, shared offices, or during lunch outings may require adjustments to your normal volume of voice.

Second, be aware of the buttons that cause you to be defensive. A clear indication of your pushed buttons is a change in your voice volume. Most workers tend to raise their voices in protest to perceived attacks, but decreasing volume level may also be noted.

Honesty is the best policy. In response to perceived attacks, state simply, "I feel like that was a personal attack towards me. Is that what you intended?" This response models I-statements and feeling statements for the client, and communicates genuineness.

**Dress**

Professional dress is a must during an interview to communicate competence and respect to a client. In addition to the common considerations of professional dress, also consider the impact of colors, wear, and accessories on the interaction. Remember that clients are making judgments about you. Expensive jewelry or complex hair styles, for example, may communicate something you do not intend to communicate.

Suffice to say, colors impact mood whether they are on the walls or on your shirt. The main point is to realize that the client is evaluating you during the interview as well. Your choice of colors speaks volumes. Darker colors can communicate a reserved quality. Brighter colors can communicate outgoing traits. Prints can communicate artistic appreciation. All black or grey can signal rejection of other points of view.

## GIM+ Introduction

Wear refers to sizing and fit of your clothing. It can also be used to discuss variations in style for men and women that frustrate standard guidelines detailing what to wear. A good example of fit is a business suit. Most would agree that a business suit suffices as professional attire. Yet, a buttoned business suit can communicate close-mindedness during an interview in the same way that a desk between worker and client signal authority. An open suit jacket or removal of the suit jacket during the interview can invite the client into conversation.

Any policy on jeans is an example of guideline frustration. Without getting into the specifics of fabric, wear, color, and cut, any policy on jeans will be inadequate. Policies on collared shirts are another example. The main consideration concerns what you intend to communicate about yourself through your dress. Be aware that whatever message will be received loud and clear by the client.

## Mannerisms

Be aware of your normal interactions with a variety of groups (e.g. friends, family, co-workers, etc.). Are you normally a person who touches others, moves your hands when you talk, is uncomfortable with silence, does not make eye contact, takes long pauses between words…the list can go on.

A common misconception is that you must throw away, re-learn, or otherwise dismiss your normal mannerisms in order to be an effective interviewer. This is not completely true. Variation in environments, needs of clients, and purpose of the interview can necessitate any of the above behaviors.

As with other considerations of tone, consider what you communicate with your mannerisms. Interacting in the most natural way will go a long way toward your ability to communicate authenticity and build rapport. Yet, your normal touching, for example, may violate a client's sense of personal space.

When you determine that your mannerisms are not congruent with the realities of the environment and the clients, utilize arrangements of the office, setting of the interview, or format (like group interview) to change the interaction.

Another option is to explain your mannerisms to the client. You may say, "My friends have told me that I touch hands and shoulders when I talk. I am going to sit facing you so that I can better respect your personal space."

**Attentiveness**

Posture, head nods, and judicious eye contact are important non-verbal conveyances of attentiveness. Increased knowledge of and experience with each client may result in differences in the utilization of non-verbal conveyances.

Posture is the key to attentiveness. GIM+ has many techniques that can communicate attentiveness during the interview process, but a posture that leans in is the single most important non-verbal method to convey interest and respect.

Nodding the head is a simple way to affirm the client. Many beginning interviewers will want to verbalize affirmation. As you will find in GIM+, verbal affirmation can be useful. But, while a client is telling a story, providing an extended answer to a question, or listing items, non-verbal nodding is most appropriate.

Eye contact is a sometimes tricky non-verbal. Judicious eye contact attempts to convey that uncertainty with the utilization of eye contact to convey attentiveness. Some clients may feel uncomfortable with extended periods of eye contact, feeling as if you are analyzing or judging them. Others may be offended by what they perceive as lack of attention as you look away at other things while they speak. Adjust based on the client's comfort.

# GIM+ Introduction

# Behaviors

### Examine Self in Relationship to the Client

You will interview clients from many different backgrounds, traditions, and socio-economic levels among other diverse characteristics. Two situations present unique challenges for the beginning interviewer. The first is when the client you will interview reminds you of yourself or reminds you of someone with whom you have conflicted relationship. Many workers find it a challenge to work with clients who remind them of mothers-in-law, spouses, high-school bullies, or other emotionally charged relationships.

The second is when the client you will interview is participating in choices or a lifestyle that you do not approve of. Consider that your first goal is to increase the client's perception of available choices. Then, empower the client to make any choice he desires. The actual choice is the client's responsibility.

### Resist Countertransference

Of course, any client that you interview is not a clone of you. The two of you may share many similarities, but one key difference is that the client has a challenge or concern that they are interested in understanding and addressing.

Rather than considering what you would do if faced with the same situation, you are tasked to follow the GIM+ change process toward identification of what the client will do to achieve her own unique goals.

Before considering a plan of action, GIM+ suggests that Engagement and Assessment occur first. Preparation is an opportunity to set that focus for yourself—to resist the tendency to solve the client's concerns as a way to address your own concerns.

### Focus on the Presenting Problem not Personal Lifestyle

As a worker, you will not agree with every choice the client makes. Being aware of this, it is important to practice self-awareness toward separating your preferences from the change process. Rather than working against the client to change their lifestyle, work with the client to address the challenge that they identify as central to the change process. The Assessment and Planning skills in GIM+ require agreement between the client and worker. Without this agreement on the goals of the interaction, the change process will be halted.

# Engagement

## Attitudes

Many beginning interviewers miss the opportunity to recognize attraction, judgment, and discrimination as important self-awareness considerations and tools of engagement. Attraction can motivate continued involvement between worker and client. Judgment allows the worker to determine the logic and consistency of the interaction. Discrimination enables the worker to distinguish between multiple options and make the most sustainable choice.

### Attraction

Perhaps one of the most misunderstood feelings among beginning interviewers is attraction. Attraction is simply the ability to draw one person to another. Attraction does not necessarily have an emotional or sexual component. The worker may use attraction as a professional behavior to draw clients toward patterns of action that may have been unattainable prior to the interaction.

### Judgment

Some have refused to make judgments about others fearing that judgment is inappropriate. To judge is to determine the logic and consistency of the interaction. Rather than making a comparison of "common sense," the professional judgment behavior in GIM+ considers what is "reasonable" from the perspective of the client.

Judgment is not a determination of right versus wrong. It is a mapping of the logic toward understanding the reasoned process of the client. It is also a determination, in concert with the client, as to whether the choices are consistent with the goals the client has for himself. The worker is judging whether the client's behavior is consistent, congruent, and authentic with the client's self-concept. When behaviors appear to be inauthentic, inconsistent, or incongruent with self-concept, the worker highlights these for client and worker to explore.

## Discrimination

Discrimination has been used as a tool of division. But to discriminate, by definition, is to distinguish between multiple options. In GIM+, we add to this definition the behavior of choosing the most sustainable choice. This behavior is especially important in the engagement skill when the client may present multiple reasons for the interview and a number of concerns that are important to her. The worker may use the professional discrimination behavior to promote a sense within the client that she is being heard.

## Competence

Competence refers to the knowledge and continued education you bring to your job. It is not enough to know the general concepts related to common mental health and behavioral issues. Competence requires a search for information in direct relationship to the individual client's profile. During the Preparation skill, you received intake information regarding the client. Continue to learn about how the individual differences of this client may impact the change process and implementation of GIM+.

### Attitudes: The Point

An attractive, married, female, 20-something intern was assigned a 16 year old, male, disconnected teen. The teen arrived in full "dark" garb, with makeup emphasizing the disconnected and "don't care" affect. The intern interacted professionally with the teen toward building rapport. She ended the interview by setting another appointment. The teen not only showed up to the subsequent appointment, he was dressed in slacks and a button-down shirt. Upon questioning, the teen admitted that he was motivated to change due to the attractiveness of the worker.

## GIM+ Introduction

# Behaviors

### Initiate Rapport

Most clients want to know who their interviewer is. Appropriate self-disclosure will be an asset throughout the interview and the entire change process. Seasoned interviewers may be able to disclose different things for different clients, but it is often useful to tell something about yourself that humanizes you in the eyes of the client. In this introduction, be sure to only disclose realities that suggest the professional resume. Purely personal disclosures such as your greatest fear or most embarrassing moments may have use during the change process, but are not appropriate as introductions. Staple disclosures include a statement of how long you have been in your current position. Another option may be to state your professional goals such as service, client well-being, or social justice.

Example: Initiate Rapport

Worker: Hi. My name is Fred Macklin. I will be interviewing you today. I have been a caseworker for 3 years. I am motivated by service and social justice. I want everyone I interview to walk away feeling that I listened. You must be Francine?

### Orient the Client to the Helping Process

Clients will arrive with varying levels of experience with change processes and agency environments. Engagement is an opportunity to orient the client to the worker as well as the process. This orienting discussion also gives the client a sense of who you are as a person and professional. Remember, just as you are assessing and self-protecting during the interaction, the client is doing the same.

### Example: Orient the Client

Worker: Before we get into our discussion, please allow me to let you know how this process works. Through our discussion, we will identify the challenges you face and your sense of the current crisis. We will build a plan of action. In later meetings, we will track the progress of our plan toward a date when you feel confident to maintain on your own. At that time, you will have the opportunity to help others.

Francine: Help others?

Worker: Yes, if you want to. We have found that successful clients are great encouragement to other clients. As well, a community of clients has a greater chance of maintaining and advancing well-being. You can help in a number of ways as simply as sharing your story or participating in a group.

## Articulate Your Professional Role

Presentation of your professional role includes 1) your purpose and intentions in the interview and 2) a statement of confidentiality—including an explanation of the limits of confidentiality. Your purpose and intentions are often set by the agency you represent. Beyond that, the professionalism embodied in GIM+ suggest that you intentionally promote service, social justice, dignity and worth of the person, the importance of human relationships, integrity and competence. When questioning whether you are making sustainable choices in the interview and change process, ask whether you are supporting your professional role—promoting professional purpose and intentions.

## Example: Professional Role

Worker: My agency is founded on the principle of community health and individual well-being. It is my goal to ensure that our discussion validates your worth, supports healthy relationships, and is honest. Does that work for you?

Francine: It does.

Worker: As a professional, I am also bound by a code of ethics to maintain the confidentiality of this interview. That means that anything you share with me will not be shared with anyone outside this agency. The only time we must break confidentiality is if you threaten another person, are planning harm to yourself, or if you make me aware of imminent danger to someone else. Do you have any questions about confidentiality?

# GIM+ Introduction

Francine: No.

### List the Agency Services

Providing information helps the client become a better consumer of services. This awareness increases options for the client and is an important ingredient in empowerment. Listing services that the agency provides is a good start toward informing the client.

### Example: Agency Services

Worker: Our agency is a health and wellness center. Our signature services include our life coaching case managers. We help with crises and connect clients to resources. Our job hunting database provides a searchable interface for finding employment based on your skills, interests, and goals. Our lifestyle health coaches assist clients with exercise, eating, and stress management plans that support healthy, balanced lifestyles.

Francine: Sounds like a great group of resources.

Worker: I'm proud of what we do. We offer a number of resources to support mental, financial, and medical health. For services that we do not offer directly, we have partnerships and referral relationships with other agencies. It's all about building a healthy community here.

### List the Client Expectations

Clients need to know both your role as interviewer and their roles as client. A clear list of client expectations is the basis for an understanding of the client role.

### Example: Client Expectations

Worker: Now you know who I am, what I do, and what the agency does. Let's talk about expectations of you as the client.

Francine: OK.

Worker: Generally, we expect you to attend appointments on time. If you are unable to make an appointment, we ask that you give us at least 24 hours of notice. We expect you to approach your interactions with staff like me honestly. Finally, we ask that you are earnest in both collaborating on your plan of action and implementing the plan of action. How do these expectations sound to you?

Francine: Each sounds doable.

## Identify the Presenting Problem

The ultimate goal of the Engagement skill is to identify the presenting problem. The presenting problem can be gained in response to a simple question, "What brings you in today?"

## Example: Presenting Problem

Worker: What brings you into the office today?

Francine: My mother suggested that I see someone for my changing moods.

## GIM+ Introduction

# Assessment

## Attitudes

### Strengths & Resilience

### Strengths

The strengths perspective is a prompt to the worker to continually look for energy and momentum presented by the client. Without a judgment of the appropriateness or sustainability of client actions, strengths perspective acknowledges the activity of the client.

To redirect energy is a much easier task than creating motivation. The strengths perspective and its recognition of the client's activity is a good starting point for encouraging internal locus of control and facilitating self-determination.

Internal Locus of control refers to the client's belief that her outcomes are due to her activity. Internal locus is contrasted with external locus, in which the client believes that the outcomes are to be blamed on others, circumstances, or fate.

Internal locus of control can be used to explain the strength of a client who puts himself into unsustainable situations wrought with unsustainable choices. If the client can see his ability to make choices, he may recognize his control over the outcomes.

Self-Determination refers to the right of every individual to make the decisions that benefit her. The value base of GIM+ also recognizes, in the context of dignity and worth of the person, that every person affirms community through their activity as an individual.

Identification of strengths facilitates self-determination by reminding the individual of both the right to choose from among available options and her possession of the abilities, skills, or resources used in making those choices. The feeling of capacity and opportunity, of self-determination in the context of strengths perspective, is also an important component of client empowerment.

## Protective Factors

The concept of protective factors is related to strengths. Protective factors are characteristics of the client's experience expressed in circumstance, capability, relationship, genetics, or belief that reduce the chance of trauma or support resilience in the face of trauma. Protective factors can be understood as biological psychological, social, spiritual, and environmental characteristics.

Biological protective factors center on the genetic characteristics that indicate a resistance to disease, accidental death, or physical deterioration. Often, assessment of biological protective factors is evident in comparison to common disease processes. For example, absence of obesity, smoking, chronic illness, disability and other obvious health risk is evidence of protective factors. The presence of risk is evidence of a lack of protective factors.

Psychological protective factors express the cognitive capacity, capability, and access of the client. Psychological protective factors also relate to the ability to process, comprehend, and act on information. Clients who are well informed are considered to have an increased number of psychological protective factors.

Social protective factors relate to the presence of human relationships that ensure access and information. Number of human relationships is only one part of the assessment. In assessing social protective factors, it is important to assess the number, role for the client, diversity of perspective, the knowledge base, and the protective factors of the human relationship cited by the client.

# GIM+ Introduction

Spiritual protective factors refer to the presence of beliefs, hope, or faith perspectives that support resilience in the client. Spiritual protective factors can be expressed in organized religions, informal relationships, habitual practices, or simple optimism.

Environmental protective factors are structural and tangible characteristics that insulate the individual from trauma. Environmental protective factors can be a function of built communities, family structure, organizational requirements, or individually constructed constraints on movement. An example of an individually constructed constraint is a personal rule to drive a certain route to work. Another example is creating a cut-off time at night for answering the phone.

## Cultural Competence

For GIM+, cultural competence begins with a view of the multi-systemic nature of client influences and the perceptions the client has of environmental helps. Multiple systems will at least include individual and family ecological systems levels. Environmental helps refer at least to reflections on community organizations and dominant culture.

## Multiple Systems

At the individual level, consider the following question: How does the client define herself? The best use of the question assesses the roles, relationships, and information that inform the client's worldview and more specifically a perception of self.

Roles can include that of mother, sister, co-worker, or writer. They define what the client is responsible for. Relationships can identify caretaker, friend, peer, or breadwinner. Relationships describe the actual responsibility in the interaction with others. Information can include parenting magazines, weekly phone calls, bulletin board, or writing professor. Information describes the sources of knowledge the client relies on in making decisions.

At the family level, consider the following question: What is the function of family? The question will illuminate elements of family structure and authority.

Generally, family structure can be patriarchal—with men deferred to as the authority—or matriarchal—with women deferred to as the authority. More specifically, family structure can describe the people who live in the home, patterns of nuclear and extended family interaction, rules, rights, privileges, and expectations expressed in the family.

Generally, authority can refer to the types of authority that are used in communication and constraining behavior. Traditionally, these types have been described as authoritative, authoritarian, or passive. More specifically, authority can describe who and what sources are valued and respected as necessary.

**Environmental Helps**

Reflections on community organizations can indicate the trust, current help seeking patterns, and potential help seeking patterns of the client. As worker, you may ask, "What organizations are comfortable for the client?" or "What organizations are uncomfortable for the client?" More than just access to organizations, the question assesses perceptions the client may have that keep him from seeking help from qualified helping agencies.

Client perceptions of the dominant culture are important. Ask the client: What stereotypes, certainties, and common sense do you accept as true? These perceptions of the dominant culture may indicate opportunities or resistance to counter culture activities. For example, if help seeking is perceived as "un-manly" or "anti-family," clients may be hesitant or reserved in an interview.

# Technique: Noting

The Noting technique has a set of 6 headings that provide order for your notes concerning the presenting problem or concerns expressed by the client. Onset refers to the origin of the concern. You may ask, "When did you become aware that this concern was something to be addressed?" or, "When did you feel that this concern was outside the norm?" Noting the onset may provide insight into an order of events and level of functioning that preceded the perception of a problem. You may follow up with the question, "What was your functioning like prior to this concern?" Or, "What was going on in your life just prior to this concern?"

**Evolution** attempts to note how the concern and its perception progressed over time. Evolution may provide insight into whether the concern has begun to impair functioning, and to what extent it has impaired functioning. This note may include information on what coping techniques have been attempted by the client, and what supportive relationships are in place. You may ask, "How has this concern changed since you first noticed it as a problem?"

**Frequency** is a simple count of occurrences of impairment. You may ask, "How often do you find this concern to be a problem for you?" Or, "How many times per week do you find yourself addressing this concern?" Noting the frequency provides insight into the amount of trauma the client may feel with this concern. Frequency noting is also information that informs Evaluation skill, specifically single-subject design and noting of intervention progress.

**Context** describes the environment, stressors, and mental states that attend the concern. Context provides insight into triggers, pathways, and patterns that may give rise to or support the concern. For environment, you may ask, "Describe where you are when you become aware of the concern?" For stressors, you may ask, "What pressures, deadlines, or anxieties do you face when the concern becomes a problem?" For mental states, you may ask, "What is typically going through your mind when you notice the concern has become a problem?" In a holistic intervention,

Context may be included in a treatment plan as a tool of sustainability. The client will learn to self-regulate and also to manipulate her environment for success.

**Intensity** notes the imperative experienced by the client during an episode of the concern or brought on by the concern. Scaling from one to ten is a useful way to ask and note intensity. You may ask, "On a scale from 1 to 10, what is the intensity of the concern (or the immediacy brought on by the concern), with 1 being 'It's not important,' and 10 being 'Life or Death'?" Depending on the concern, the phrasing of the 1 and 10 descriptions can be changed. Noting intensity can provide insight in the client's ability to think rationally during an episode. Rational thinking is important for self-regulation. If Intensity is unmanageable, it will be important to include interventions to reduce intensity added to those that proactively address the concern.

**Duration** of Episodes notes the length of the episode or concern brought on by the episode. You may ask, "How long does a typical episode last?" Or, "How much time passes before you can return to what you consider a normal level of functioning?" Noting Duration of Episodes may provide insight into potential patterns of intervention or habits to practice. As with other numeric representations of the concern, decreases in Duration of Episodes can be used to demonstrate progress in the intervention.

# Behaviors

The Assessment skill in GIM+ has two behaviors: Probing and Reflecting. The Assessment skill also has one technique: Noting. Probing extends the conversation. Reflecting makes sense of the conversation. Noting provides a template for noting the presenting problems and client concerns.

# GIM+ Introduction

## Probing

Probing behavior includes two tasks questioning and prompting. **Questioning** is perhaps the most common of tasks utilizing natural curiosity to form simple questions.

### Example: Questioning

Worker: When did you notice that you were having moods?

Francine: We just buried my dad three weeks ago. I have been in a funk since then. I haven't been able to focus at work.

Worker: Is this funk affecting other areas of your life?

Francine: I would say I am kind of depressed when I'm home, moping around, sleeping a lot. At work, I am forgetting assignments, and generally not feeling motivated.

## Prompting

It may be helpful to think of prompting as "connecting the dots" in the conversation. When a client presents information, prompting allows the worker to put the pieces together and cluster information.

### Example: Prompting

Worker: Your moods are stemming from having buried your father? Have you talked to anyone about grief counseling?

Francine: No. It seems like I haven't had time to do anything but take care of the basics.

## Reflecting

Reflecting behavior includes four tasks: Clarifying, Partializing, Paraphrasing, and Interpreting Meaning. **Clarifying** attempts to establish definitions of concepts agreed upon between the worker and client.

## Example: Clarifying

Francine: She had a "canipsy" when she didn't get her way.

Worker: A canipsy?

Francine: Yeah. She got really upset and started beating her fists on the floor.

Worker: So, canipsy is a temper tantrum?

Francine: …a bad one.

Francine: It's really tragic that the world has gotten so liberal.

Worker: Liberal?

Francine: Yeah. It's like everyone thinks that you can leave your kids with daycares and babysitters instead of taking care of them.

Worker: So, liberal means allowing others to take care of your child?

Francine: …instead of taking care of them yourself.

**Partializing** is all about listing the elements of the client's presentation that are actionable. Clients will often present contextual information, anecdotes, and other ancillary information that provides a fuller picture of their situation. Not all this information is useful for interpreting the interview and planning action steps. In partializing, the worker breaks up what the client is saying into a list of potential actions. When in crisis, it may be difficult for the client to see the distinctions between one idea and another. The worker, in delineating a list of the ideas parsed, supports a sense of clarity needed for client coping.

## Example: Partializing

Francine: There is so much going on with my father's death, losing my job, my daughter starting kindergarten, and getting my mother's affairs in order. It's going to be a new thing for her living on her own. I don't know whether I should move in with her or what. She and my father were so close. You know, they were married for more than 35 years?

# GIM+ Introduction

Worker: So, it sounds like we have grief issues, concerns about the job situation, concerns about your daughter starting school, and living arrangements for mom?

Francine: I need to get a new job, and get my mother and daughter situated.

Worker: How are you coping with your father's passing?

Francine: I'm just staying busy... It's not working well though.

Worker: Perhaps our list of actions should include job hunting, mother's living arrangements, your daughter's school, and your grief work?

Francine: If you can help.

**Paraphrasing** is a simple demonstration that you hear what the client has said. Paraphrasing often seems patronizing to the beginning interviewer, but clients feel heard when you are able to repeat to them what they have said.

## Example 1: Paraphrasing

Francine: My father's death really took me off guard. I am usually a together type of person, but this was tough.

Worker: Sounds like you are normally a tough person, but your father's death really took you off guard.

Francine: It still hurts.

## Example 2: Paraphrasing

Francine: I'm not sure what options are available for grief work. I just know I don't have time to see some shrink twice a week.

Worker: It sounds like you aren't sure what options for grief work exist, and you want something less than twice a week.

Francine: Yes. This once every two weeks is bad enough.

**Interpreting Meaning** tests the worker's perception of what the client is saying. Before proceeding to the Planning skill, the information gained in Assessment must be crystalized into a list of actions AND a shared sense of what the performance of those actions makes possible. Together, this list of actions and shared sense of potential is client meaning. This sense of meaning potentially results in self-sufficiency.

### Example 1: Interpreting Meaning

Worker: If we can outline a plan for job hunting, a schedule for transitioning your daughter into school, a goal for your mother's care, and a bi-weekly grief recovery group, how balanced do you think you will be on a scale from 1 to 10, 10 being perfectly balanced.

Francine: If we can get all that accomplished, I should be at a 10, very balanced and able to be me again.

### Example 2: Interpreting Meaning

Worker: It seems that your father's death has really upset your normal coping. Does this seem the case to you?

Francine: I didn't realize it until this talk, but dad's death has been the common thread in my stress and the funk I have been in. I was fine right up until the funeral, but after that…I don't know.

GIM+ Introduction

# Planning

## Attitudes

### Client Primacy

Client Primacy refers to an attitude of respect, interest, and partnership in relationship to the achievement of client goals. After all, client success is evaluated through the eyes of the client, not the worker. Client primacy also promotes client motivation.

### Respect

Client primacy suggests a practical respect for the client's approaches, experiences, and perceptions of the challenges she faces. Consider that the client knows more about the actual moment-by-moment occurrences, players, and situations even when in crisis. The client's ability to make sense of and formulate responses to the crisis may be impaired, but she has a view of the crisis that should be respected. Value the elements that are communicated by the client.

### Interest

In assessment, you found out about the client. The client may have addressed similar difficulties in the past. This experience is important to both promoting success in the current crisis, and identifying challenges in the current crisis that may require additional coping skills. A successful worker will be open to past coping experience and skillful in suggesting additional coping options.

### Partnership

Partnership suggests that the change process is collaborative. A typical written plan for the client may only indicate activities that will be performed by the client. But, consider that the worker will perform some activities as well. It is important for the client to complete the change process having gained self-sufficiency skills, but the modeling and support of those skills may come first from the worker.

### Motivation

Achieving success in a change process is often credited to internal motivation and perseverance, but an important place exists for the external motivation of the worker. Skillful planning will result in a change process with achievements that inspire the client to attempt tougher activities. Assurance from the worker increases the chances that the client will take appropriate risks toward her goals.

### Data-based Action Plan & Client Agreement

**Coping** options are best presented in the context of the data obtained during the assessment. Connecting goal development in this way ensures that the logic of the goal can be traced by the client. This ability to trace the logical creation of a goal further supports the client's ability to create solutions during future crises.

### Self-sufficiency

If the client can be supported to develop goals, the pattern can be replicated during the next crisis. Skillful planning not only produces a plan, but models a systematic approach to organizing the change process. In addition to agreement with the plan, the worker does well to ensure client's awareness of the planning process itself.

## Technique: Evaluate Goal Structure

Goals have to be SMART: Specific, Measurable, Attainable, Relevant, and Time Oriented.

**Specific** hearkens back to the Interpret Meaning behavior within the Assessment skill. To make a goal specific is to articulate the connection between the goal and the purpose of those goals. The client should be able to articulate the coping or change that will result from the completing the goal.

**Measurable** goals have waypoints—the how—built into them. Measurable goals can be observed as achieved or not-achieved. Amounts, dates, counts or other observable criteria may support the construction of measurable goals.

**Attainable** goals have a strategy evident in how they are expressed. The client must perceive the strategy as achievable in the environment in which she lives. The client perception can be influenced by attitudes, finances, prior trauma, and other people. Often, creating attainable goals involves engaging the client to see beyond the current crisis and perceive what his behaviors (and perceptions) would be if the current crisis were resolved.

**Relevant** goals are a direct result of a proper Assessment and Planning. Relevant goals are goals that the client believes will result in a change the client desires. Relevant goals are also properly matched with services available or properly resourced.

**Time-Oriented** goals include a time limit or a time consideration. Time-oriented goals are not always ending times. They can be expressed as periodic review times, in which the worker may interact with the client to evaluate progress.

## Behaviors

The Planning Skill has 3 behaviors: Connect with Services, Translate Into Goals, and Contract with Client. The Planning skill also has one technique that suggest best practices for change process planning: Evaluating Goal Structure.

### Connect with Services

Connecting with Services is an extension of the Partializing behavior conducted in the Assessment skill. Remember that Partializing identifies the actionable elements. Partializing refers to an ability to separate the various ideas and concerns expressed by the client. Once the conversation is parsed, determine the most important ideas and concerns. With actionable elements identified, **Connect with Services** now connects the available services with the needs of the client. Be sure to make an explicit record of the client needs and the services connected to enable follow-up.

### Example: Connect with Services

Worker: Perhaps our list of actions should include job hunting, mother's living arrangements, your daughter's school, and your grief work?

Francine: If you can help.

Worker: As a health and wellness center, we have a number of resources for mental, financial, and medical health including partnerships and referral relationships. For job hunting, we have a database accessible in our computer lab that lists local employment opportunities. We have a relationship with an elder care facility that offers consultation specifically for widows and widowers that may fit the needs of your mother. Our agency is one of the "Back to School" partners along with the school district. I am sure we can help you facilitate the transition of your daughter. We also have life coaches on staff. One, in particular, runs a grief support group.

Francine: Okay. I'm in the right place then.

### Translate Into Goals

**Translate Into Goals** is all about timing. Rarely is the real world linear and amenable to doing one thing at a time. The skillful worker must gauge and agree with the client on how best to reach homeostasis with goals that can be understood individually, but implemented as an integrated whole. Sometimes, the ability to achieve one goal depends on the achievement of another goal. When this is the case, the worker must order goals accordingly. It is important to outline goals that are immediate or near immediate to implement and contrast them with goals that typically require more steps and a longer implementation period. Be sure to support self-sufficiency by challenging the client to create goals with your assistance.

### Example: Translate Into Goals

## GIM+ Introduction

Worker: Let us outline a set of goals. I'll create one goal to show you how it's done. You can then create others.

Francine: Okay. Let's do it.

Worker: Goal one… I will complete the 6-week grief group curriculum with no more than 1 absence.

Francine: How often does it meet?

Worker: It's once per week, on Thursday evenings, 7:00pm.

Francine: That's doable.

Worker: You try.

Francine: Goal two…I will attend the parent orientation event at my daughter's school and complete the registration paperwork provided there.

Worker: You have a date for that?

Francine: Sure. It's always the 3rd Wednesday in July, 9:00am to 5:00pm.

Worker: Great!

Francine: I got it. These goals rock!

Worker: Are they going to be doable?

Francine: Sure.

## Contract with the Client

The change process hinges upon gaining agreement with the client about the reality that they perceive and about the goals that they are motivated to achieve. Contracting is a behavior that solidifies the commitment between the worker and the client. In fee-for-service relationships, contracting can include agreement to pay for services and continue toward goal achievement. In all relationships, contracting provides a paper trail of goal setting and client agreement.

**Example: Contract with Client**

Worker: Francine, this is a print out of the 4 goals we have identified. I would like for you to read each of them aloud, and mark your agreement with each. Once you are done reading, please sign it and date. I will sign and date also.

Francine: Thanks.

GIM+ Introduction

# Implementation

## Attitudes

### Empowerment: Permission, Perspective & Options

Empowerment refers to a process of change specifically focusing on the identification of strengths that become action. Four-components of empowerment exist: resources, decision points, structural controls, and experience.

Resources refer to money, information, people, and time. Access to these resources is supportive of empowerment in clients. Clients without access or limited access to these resources have diminished opportunities to act on personal strengths.

**Resource** empowerment is the activity of the worker to increase access for the client. It may also involve practicing with the client to increase a sense of permission (as compared to entitlement).

The phrase "**decision points**" describes the moments at which options must be acted upon. Though a plan is created, action requires decision making. If a client is empowered, she must recognize the moments that offer opportunity to initiate choice. She also recognizes the implications of one choice compared to another choice.

"**Structural controls**" refers to an awareness of the mechanisms that serve to transfer and constrain the transmission of culture. The empowered individual believes that he impacts culture through his choices. He is also aware of the norms and beliefs that he internalizes as well as the protocols and practices to which he adapts.

Empowerment **experience** is the ability to act gained from the access, perspective, and awareness identifying strengths that become action. The empowered client, then, makes the choice that gets her closer to her goals.

Assessment of empowerment includes each of the four components above.

## Behaviors

The Implementation Skill has six behaviors: Focusing, Advising, Representing, Reframing, Confronting, and Responding with Immediacy.

**Focusing**

**Focusing** maintains the attention of the client on the plan that has been developed. Often, the incremental success of a change process may lead to a feeling that the worst is over, and the process can conclude. Alternatively, some clients may decide that, in consultation with other people, they would like to augment or supplement the plan created. It is difficult to know for certain whether these proposed changes are a signal of increased self-determination and the ability of the client to cope or less sustainable reasoning. Focusing seeks to integrate the client's perceptions into the course of the current plan. It may be that a new plan needs to be constructed. In this case, create a completely new plan returning to the Planning Skill. Resist the pressure or inclination to modify the current plan without the professional habits of the skill and evaluation of structure technique. Piece-meal modifications can result in poor outcomes, unintended consequences, and an inability to monitor outcomes effectively.

**Example: Focusing**

Francine: I was talking with my mother, and she thinks I shouldn't work. I should just focus on raising my daughter especially now that she is in school. Should we modify that part?

Worker: Our plan outlined the sense of purpose and satisfaction you feel from working. Plus, we discussed your excitement about putting in some hours while your daughter is at school…staying busy. We can build a new plan, but modifying this upsets other satisfactions we built into the plan.

Francine: That makes sense. We can't just break apart a plan that was built for my success.

# GIM+ Introduction

## Advising

**Advising** capitalizes on the ongoing results of implementing a plan. Clients will find that their view of the options available to them increases. Advising uses this realization to offer more and varied options to the client. Advising also empowers the client to consider and make sustainable choices.

### Example 1: Advising

Francine: I am having some trouble finding employment leads. The paper doesn't seem to have any good options.

Worker: Have you checked the employment database here at the center?

Francine: No…How do I get connected with that?

Worker: Let me connect you with Margarite over in the computer lab. She can set you up.

### Example 2: Advising

Francine: I spent some time looking on the employment database. There are 6 options that are just for me. There are 8 that I may need some help with.

Worker: Share with me what help you feel you need.

Francine: I just don't know about filling applications out online.

Worker: I'll walk with you through one. You'll see that it's not too bad, and that will increase your prospects to 14 positions!

## Representing

**Representing** combines roles of broker, advocate, and negotiator to assist clients in areas where they need collaboration or areas where they have not established a voice. In brokering, clients may not have attempted a conversation before and require the worker to set up an interaction.

In advocacy, a client may have been denied services or access, and she may need the worker to make a phone call or compose a letter on her behalf. In negotiation, the client may not have the skills to communicate his position to another party, and he needs the worker to demonstrate the skill with the other party on his behalf.

### Example: Representing

Francine: I encountered one job application that required that I have a reference from an employment counselor. Do you know what I can do about that?

Worker: We have that designation here. All our workers can compose those letters for you to include in your employment package.

Francine: Great! I'll get on the application then.

### Reframing

**Reframing** is a particularly useful behavior when a client is faced with setbacks in the course of plan implementation. Reframing introduces a new way of thinking about a situation that motivates action rather than confirming despair. Reframing emphasizes that more than one interpretation exists for every occurrence.

### Example: Reframing

Francine: I have put in 4 applications. Only one job called me. I went to the interview, but they didn't give me the job.

Worker: How long has it been?

Francine: It's been two weeks. The others should have called by now. And, I still don't understand why I didn't get that job I interviewed for.

Worker: Remember, job interviews are not just an evaluation of your employability, they are also an evaluation of your fit with the company. Sometimes, you may not fit for the company.

Francine: I guess…and the hours weren't the best for my responsibilities.

# GIM+ Introduction

Worker: Our plan states that we will evaluate progress after a month. Two weeks is time, but let's keep working this part of the plan throughout evaluation date at the end of the month.

Francine: Let's do it. I guess it helps to keep working the plan.

## Confronting

**Confronting** is a difficult behavior for many beginning interviewers. The key to effective confronting is to focus on the unsustainable behaviors and point out the other options available to the client. In this way, the worker resists the judgment of the client. The judgment is focused on the behavior.

## Example: Confronting

Worker: You identified 14 potential jobs in the database. We worked together to reduce that to 10. Yet, you only applied for 4 positions. Help me to understand this?

Francine: I didn't feel like the others were a good fit once I got on their website.

Worker: Yet, we compared your prior work experience and interests to the job descriptions. What else is going on here?

Francine: I just didn't feel that I could do it. They looked way over my head.

Worker: You must still apply. It's what we agreed to in our plan. Better still, apply and get the job before you disqualify yourself.

## Responding with Immediacy

**Responding with Immediacy** is a behavior primarily concerned with relationship maintenance between the client and the worker. It may be helpful to set up a contact schedule so that the client knows when she can expect you to return phone calls, respond to email, schedule meetings, and be unavailable. During Implementation, contact is important. "Responding with immediacy" means never leaving a client without someone to call. It does not mean that you personally are available for the client 24 hours a day, 7 days per week. Ideally, the resource you provide to the client, should she need to call for help, are resources that are available even after the change process has terminated. In this way, the client has a greater chance of maintaining the successes gained during the change process.

**Example: Responding with Immediacy**

Worker: Should you have any concerns that I can help with during your job search, feel free to call me between 4:00pm and 5:00pm weekdays. If I am on another call, please leave a message. I'll return the call usually before I leave that day, or first thing in the morning.

Francine: I don't like leaving messages on machines.

Worker: It's the only way for me to know that I need to return the call.

Francine: What if it's an emergency?

Worker: We do have a hotline here for 24/7 emergencies. Call that number, and you will have a worker on the line that can help.

GIM+ Introduction

# Evaluation

## Attitudes

### Reflecting on Practice with the Client

Reflecting with the client provides one further opportunity to remind the client of her successes and the skills learned during the change process. The goal is always to support the client's ability to recognize imbalances, identify coping options, cope using more immediate supports, and promote protective factors that are sustainable. Reflection with the client should aid this awareness.

Reflect with the client on how she recognizes stress. Remind the client of the stress coping techniques she has learned and utilized throughout the change process. Suggest common causes of stress and resources within her family and other systems that may offer assistance. Provide the client with a list of agency resources that can be accessed if the need for additional help arises. Remind the client that she has succeeded using these resources in the past. Past success suggests success in the future.

### Contribute to the Professional Knowledge Base

Consider that the techniques you have practiced with your current client may be useful to other professionals. If you can show evidence of success for a specific approach to practice, other professionals can build upon your success to assist other clients in their change processes. Systematic evaluation aids the process of sharing what may be termed evidence-based practice.

Many beginning workers are hesitant to share evaluations of practice because it opens the worker to critique from other professionals, or because writing is required.

In order to handle the stress of being critiqued, lean on the GIM+ process and the individual differences of your specific client. Approach the sharing as evaluation of the GIM+ process itself. Careful attention to behaviors that are more or less useful provides insight into improvements in technique for you and other workers utilizing the change process.

Each client presents with different amounts of motivation, introspection, capacity, and resources. Your experience as a worker does reflect on you, but it also reveals differences based in the client that may be learned from in preparation for similar clients.

In order to address any fears or perceive inadequacies in writing, consider recording your evaluation with an audio recorder. A recorded interview with a supervisor or colleague can also be a useful prompt with questions that spur deeper analysis of the case. Transcripts of this interaction can be edited for sharing.

Research reports are another way to share outcomes. The reports can be used to provide examples, create trainings, or to review progress. Single-subject design is a research method well suited for evaluation of a single client interaction.

## Technique: Single-Subject Design

Evaluation during an interview can provide you with opportunity to coach, confront, or congratulate during that interview. Single-subject design is a technique that can utilize the comparison of scaling responses across interview sessions to indicate progress overtime or efficacy of certain interventions. Single-subject design works well with the Noting Technique and Scaling behavior highlighted in this title.

Consider that if you ask certain specific scaling questions over a period of time, say four weeks, you can evaluate whether the client is progressing, fluctuating, or declining. Note the responses to the scaling questions, along with the questions, for this individual client. Progressing each of the four weeks with increasing numbers could indicate that the plan is

## GIM+ Introduction

working—no need to change anything. Fluctuating with higher numbers one week and lower numbers the next could indicate a lack of focus or inconsistencies that can be addressed. Declining with lower numbers each of four weeks could indicate that a new plan needs to be created, one that fits better with the assessment. It may also indicate that the assessment of the client was flawed. In this case, a new assessment and plan should be considered.

## Behaviors

Evaluation has one behavior: Scaling.

### Scaling

**Scaling** can be used in multiple ways that make it useful in periodic monitoring of client activity. Scaling is a fairly simple assessment of the client on a continuum. Commonly, the continuum is from 1 to 10. The worker assigns a value to 1 and a value to 10. The client then rates herself on that continuum.

### Example: Scaling Continuum

Worker: On a scale from 1 to 10, 10 being the best interview ever, 1 being a complete waste of time, please rate this interview.

Francine: I would have to say it's a 10. I have no complaints.

Scaling can focus on Goal-Attainment, Task-Achievement, or Target Problem. Think of the planning of goals with tasks as components of those goals. You may have 1 or more tasks for each goal. By completing the tasks, the client is progressing toward completing the goal. In Goal-Attainment Scaling, the worker is assessing how thoroughly the goal has been completed including the purpose and outcome expectations included in the goal.

### Example: Goal-Attainment Scaling

Worker: On a scale from 1 to 10, 1 being "nothing satisfied" and 10 being "everything worked," where would you rate our goal for getting a job?

Francine: I would have to say a 7. It's not my dream job, but it does fit the hours I wanted and my interests.

In Task Achievement Scaling, the worker can periodically assess progress on tasks. This can provide opportunity to coach, confront, or congratulate the client. Progress on tasks equals progress on goals.

**Example: Task-Achievement Scaling**

Worker: On a scale from 1 to 10, 1 being "not compliant at all" and 10 being "fully compliant," rate your compliance with our job application task.

Francine: 10, my friend. I have completed all the applications we outlined. What's more, I have attended all the interviews that I got scheduled.

In Target-Problem Scaling, the worker is seeking to assess the client's amount of anxiety or "feeling in crisis" at a given time. In addition to the more mechanical process of tasks and goals, it may be important to gauge how the client feels about the process and her progress toward well-being. Target-Problem Scaling can get at this information effectively.

**Example: Target-Problem Scaling**

Worker: I know you have been putting in a lot of work, and you have made some real progress in my eyes. On a scale from 1 to 10, 1 being "minimal progress" and 10 being "more progress than I thought possible," rate your progress in addressing you reason for coming to the agency.

Francine: Hmmm. I haven't really thought about this, but I know I am making some progress. I don't feel the same paralysis, not knowing what to do. I would say 6, maybe 7.

# GIM+ Introduction

# Termination

## Attitudes

### Sensitivity to Emotional Attachment

Effective interviewers are often characterized by the ability to attach. Letting go of the attachment is not always the easiest task. Effective termination includes the ability to anticipate the end point of the interaction and prepare for the sense of loss that attends termination.

### Reflecting on Practice with Colleagues

The endpoint of your interactions with clients offers a grand opportunity to reflect on your interviewing practice. Supervision with a seasoned interviewer should be a part of ongoing practice. Reflection with other interviewers, your colleagues, can also be an important part of development once a professional interaction is concluded. Reflection with peers can include an analysis of the use of GIM+ step-by-step. Your change process in specific environments or with specific populations may not exactly fit the linear steps of the GIM+ model. Discussions with colleagues can crystalize specific instructions for implementing the model that are specific to your environment and population.

## Behaviors

Termination has four behaviors: Make Referral or Trans-ferral, Plan for Termination, Articulate Goal Completion, Complete Final Evaluation.

### Make Referral

Referral and Trans-ferral are terms that concern connecting the client with additional consultation, services, and expertise. Referral refers to connections made outside the agency set of services. Trans-ferral refers to connections with staff within the agency set of services.

### Plan for Termination

Plan for Termination includes the tasks of reviewing the process and keeping goals forefront. These tasks will guide every discussion with clients. In the initial Engagement Skill, the worker orients the client to the process of helping. Every subsequent interaction updates the client to the current stage of the change process.

## Reviewing the Process

The client's awareness of the change process including schedules, supports available, and opportunities to challenge her are important to maintain. Each intends to communicate the time-limited nature of the current change process as well as the community-centered independence of the client—that is, crisis is not perpetual. Coping and success is a lifestyle within the community, not just a result of dealing with crisis.

"**Schedules**" concerns whether the waypoints of the change process are being achieved as expected. Making the client aware of this further demystifies the change process and provides a greater chance that the client can cope without help. Along the way, the client will have hurdles to overcome. Providing resources beyond the worker and beyond the agency are important to establishing a sense of a community of support for the client. Often, the hurdles offer an opportunity for the client to challenge her conceptions of her own ability, her expectations, and her view of her past. The worker can point out these opportunities and demonstrate to the client a process of dealing with challenges as opportunities.

## Keeping Goals Forefront

It is common for beginning interviewers to establish rapport with relative ease and have greater trouble with the documentation of progress. One way to address this challenge is to begin each interaction with the client by reviewing the change process goals. Each interaction with the client may end with homework based on an action related to a goal. In this way, goals are placed in the forefront of the interaction. Progress can be noted through the Noting technique and further expressed in the responses to scaling questions.

# GIM+ Introduction

## Example: Plan for Termination

Worker: Francine, this is our 3rd interaction, and you have been making a great deal of progress with the goals we have set. You were able to get the job quicker than we anticipated. Your daughter is in school. And, you are working with your mom to get her affairs in order.

Francine: Yes, I guess it has been moving along.

Worker: On a scale from 1 to 10, 1 being "in crisis", and 10 being "coping well," what would you give your current state of crisis compared to when we first interacted?

Francine: I have to give it an 8. I still have some work to do related to my father's passing. In the group last week, I noticed how adjusted others were in comparison to me. A couple of them assured me that I could get there though.

Worker: That's good to hear. Even though we are nearing the end of this goal plan, you may continue with the grief counseling. In addition, the connections you have made with the education program and the elder care program are community supports that will continue to be available to you.

Francine: That's good to know. I didn't know I had that many resources right in my community.

## Articulate Goal Completion

Once goals are completed, the change process is over. Your final interaction with the client can be used to re-emphasize the strengths of the client and the mechanism of follow-up employed by the agency. If your agency employs a pre-post survey, you may administer the instrument.

Success in the GIM+ is measured by the client's awareness of his strength and ability to cope in the face of subsequent crises. To this end, the final interaction of the plan is used to evaluate the extent to which the client recognizes the success as his. A worker can walk with the client through the list of goals and ask the client how he would cope with the same challenge if faced with it again. Scaling questions can be added to gauge the client's confidence in his ability.

**Example: Articulate Goal Completion**

Worker: Hi, Francine. Welcome to our final interaction concerning this goal plan.

Francine: It's hard to believe it's actually coming to an end.

Worker: And you have done it.

Francine: Not without help.

Worker: Yes, but we all need help. That's what our final interaction is all about. We are going to walk through out list of goals, describe your success, and gauge your confidence in dealing with that crisis again on a scale…

Francine: …from 1 to 10. More scaling questions, eh?

Worker: Yes, more scaling questions.

Francine: Let's do it.

Worker: First, you searched our employment database, connected with potential jobs. You determined a set of 12 to go after. You applied, even to the ones that were online. You went on interviews. And, finally, you landed a job.

Francine: Yes. I overcame a few fears in that process.

Worker: On a scale from 1 to 10, 1 being "can't handle it" and 10 being "simple as following directions," how confident are you that you could find and secure another job if you needed to?

Francine: 10. No question. It's hard to see what my hesitation was back then. I'm good with my job now, but I do have my resume on an employment website, and I browse for other jobs as a way to deal with stress at work.

Worker: Great. I'll check that one off. Next…

# GIM+ Introduction

## Complete Final Evaluation

The final evaluation is the wrap-up to any evaluation reporting, single-subject designs, or other research being conducted with the client. Even if no formal research was constructed, it is a good practice to enter a final comment on the lessons learned for each client. These comments may be an effective starting point for the creation of case studies, trainings, or best practices manuals.

# Follow-up

## Attitudes

### "No-Exit" Relationships

The idea of "no-exit" or long-term follow-up supports two primary capacity building exercises for the interviewing organization: long-term impact evaluation and creation of a support pool.

### Resource for Evaluating Long-term Impact

Clients who have completed the change process are an important resource as an ongoing case study and evaluation opportunity. As a case study, the day-to-day activities, resilience, psychological, social, and environmental influences on the client can be instructive about the effect of the change process in the long-term. Success stories can be presented in promotional materials as well as used as examples to motivate current change interactions.

A review of case studies, even as cross-sectional snapshots, provides the ability to compare the success of clients over time. Specific process changes, worker reflections, and community changes can be combined with a time-specific review of client outcomes to suggest how those changes impact client outcomes. This long-term impact study offers information that is invaluable to organizational development.

### Support Pool for Current & Future Clients

Clients who are successful in the change process may be valuable sources of support for current clients. Hearing the concepts, encouragement, uncertainties, and stories of perseverance from peers can be a powerful supplement to formal GIM+ interactions. Many implementations of this support utilize technology for secure and discrete, ongoing engagement.

## Behaviors

Follow-up in GIM+ ensures benefit for the client and the worker. The client benefits from the creation of a "sponsor" relationship—a

## GIM+ Introduction

relationship initiated, monitored, or validated by the agency that supports continued coping success. The worker benefits from the learning gained from the creation of a training case based on the experience with the client.

### Sponsor Relationship

GIM+ extends typical practice in social interviews by suggesting that the relationship initiated in the interview continue into perpetuity. This arrangement can be accomplished by connecting the client to ongoing-support groups or community entities such as churches, clubs, senior centers, or other civic groups. Consider that the agency can support the continued coping success of clients by ensuring the continuation of effective sponsor organizations in the community.

### Create Training Case

Interactions with clients, however brief, produce information that can be helpful in training other workers or improving the insight and practice of the attending worker. In creating a training case, at least four areas present opportunities for learning: major challenges, process learning, self-learning, and lessons for other workers.

Major challenges experienced by the worker and the client can provide insight into needed policies, information, services, or agency relationships. An awareness of these challenges may provide continuous quality improvement for the agency as well as the worker. It may also indicate targets for advocacy beyond the agency.

Process learning refers to a consideration of the best way to accomplish a task. In hindsight, easier paths to an outcome may be clear. In this analysis, it is important for the worker to consider the stress and pressures that contributed to the selection of a certain path selection. Process learning is part recognition of a different path and part planning to address the stress and pressures. Often, a more sustainable choice is harder to see in the moment than it appears in hindsight.

Self-learning refers to insight the worker gains about herself as a result of considering the interactions with the client. Many beginning workers are surprised with the possessiveness they exhibit with clients. Taking responsibility for a client is appropriate. Behaving as if you are the only person alive that can help the client is not appropriate. References to "my clients" as opposed to "our clients" may indicate the need for appropriate responsibility training. Beginning workers may also have trouble separating out tasks for the client to attempt versus those that the worker can more effectively undertake. Self-learning may include exploring whether the challenge is too great for the client versus the need of the worker to "help" while denying the client the opportunity to attempt, fail, and learn.

"Lessons for other workers" refers to general awareness or considerations that could be of benefit to all workers in the agency. A common realization is the need for a resource manual listing available community agencies for referral, resources, or sponsorship. Other lessons may include specific considerations about a certain population of clients, specifics about a region, or agency services or evidence-based practices that came online after the case was concluded.